Who I belong to:

Between Ezra And The Key

Written and Illustrated by: Garet & Andrea Krane

MEET THE CHARACTERS

EZRA THE HIPPOPOTAMUS

EZRA THE GRASSHOPPER

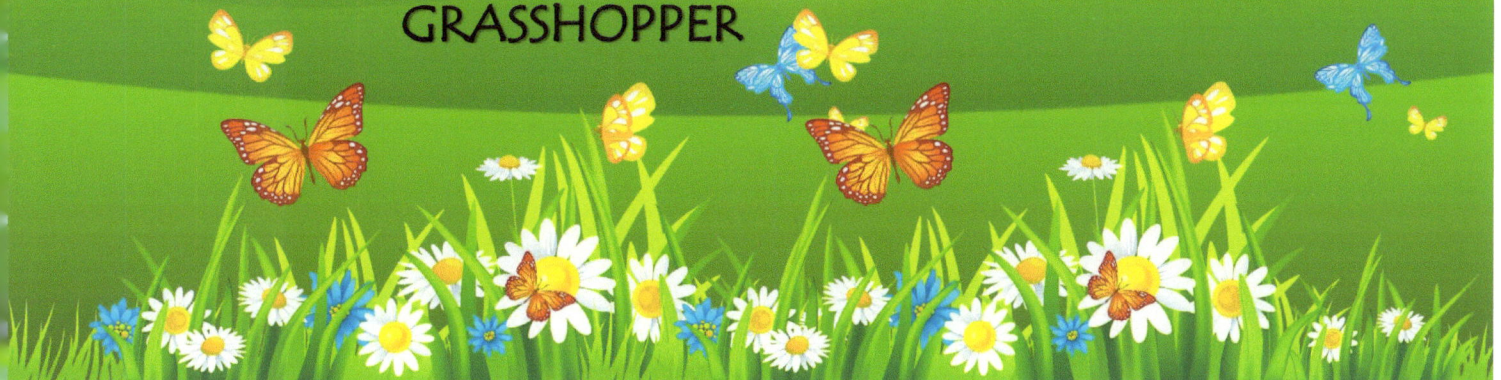

EZRA THE COW

One day a young boy was standing in class,

He was looking at the clock watching the time pass.

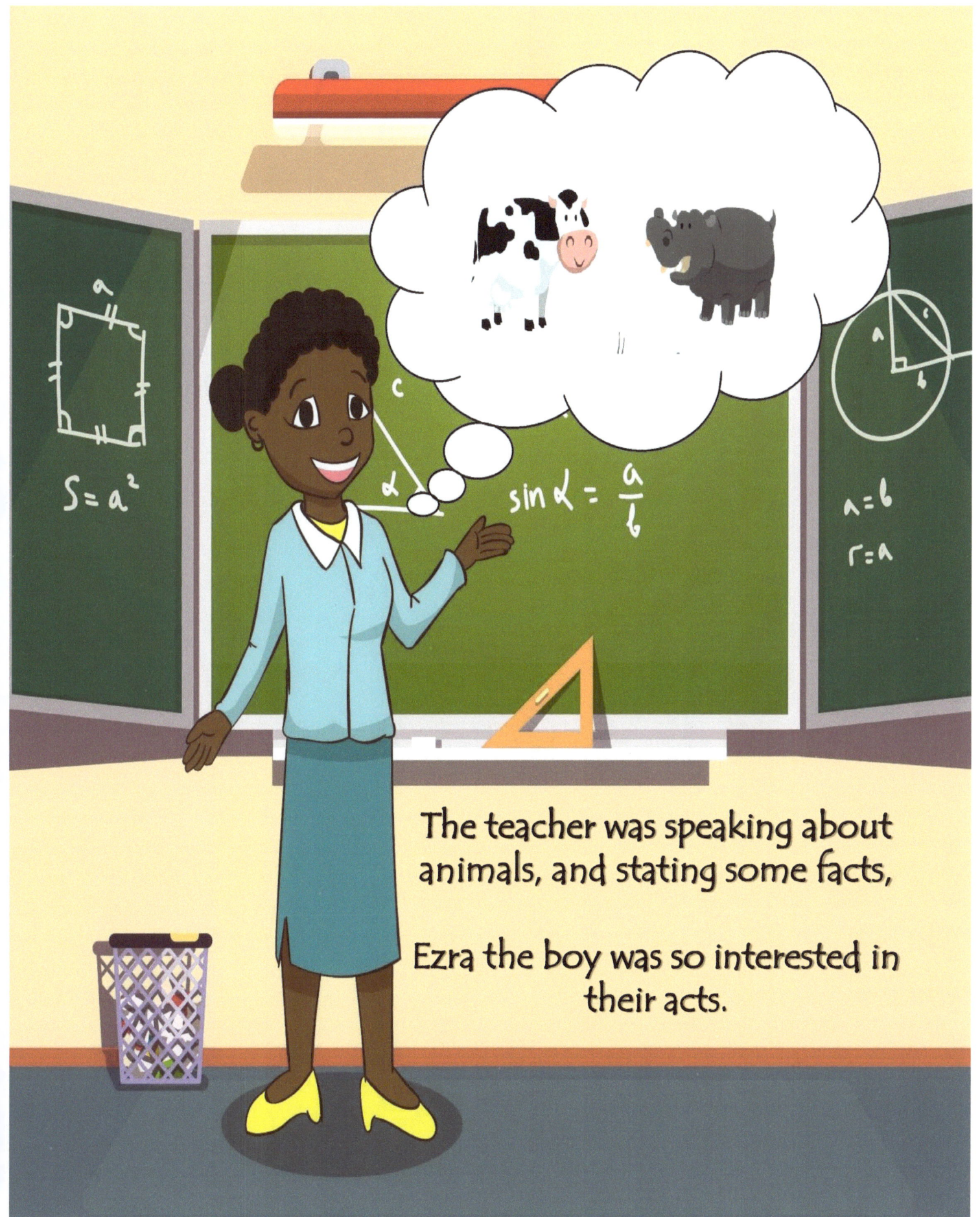

The teacher was speaking about animals, and stating some facts,

Ezra the boy was so interested in their acts.

Ezra started
to daydream…

What would it be like in
their shoes?

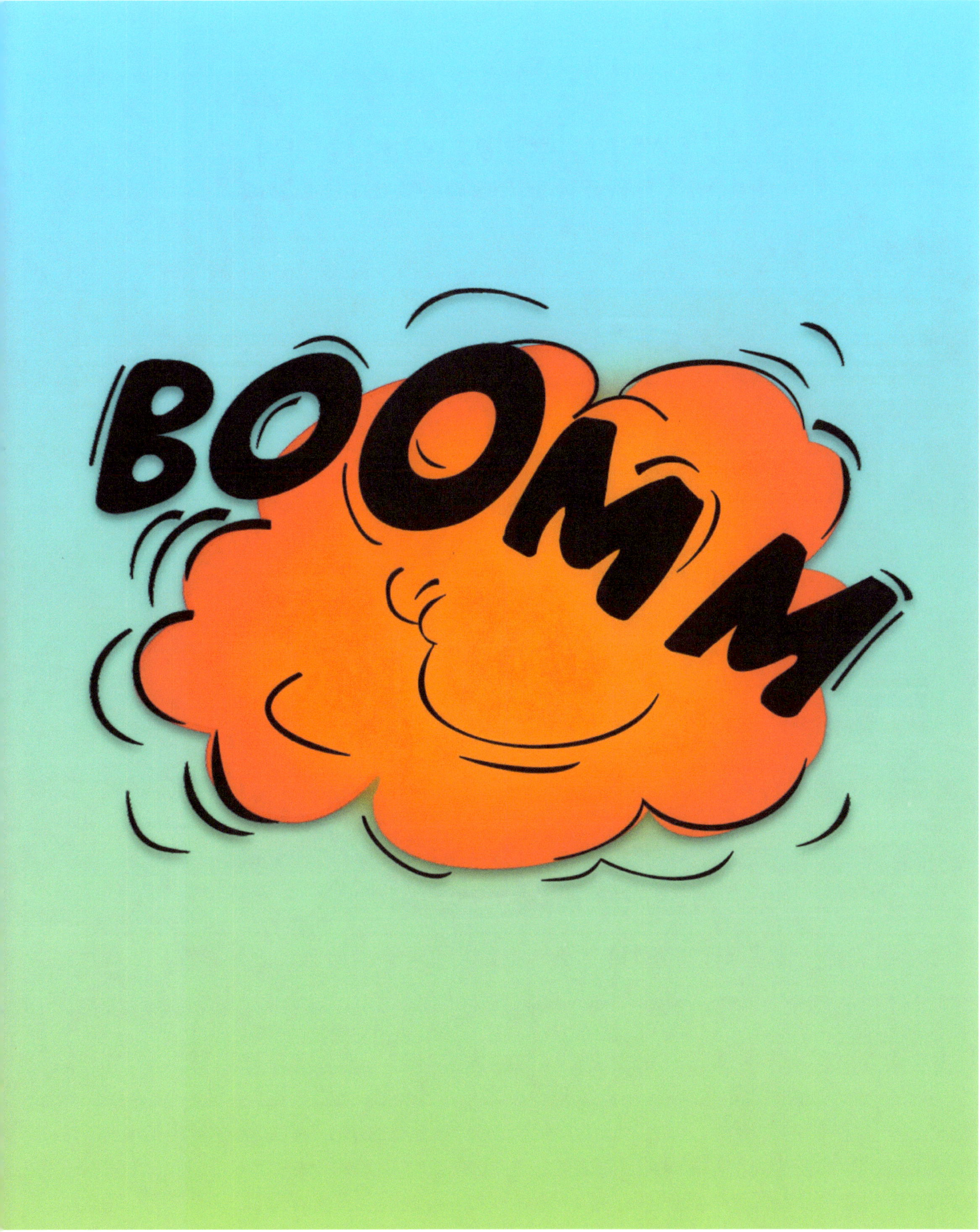
BOOMM

"It's weird sleeping while I stand,
I don't have fingers or even a hand."

Ezra is now a cow.

What is even stranger is that cows can only dream laying down,

Cows are more than black and white, they are even red, and brown.

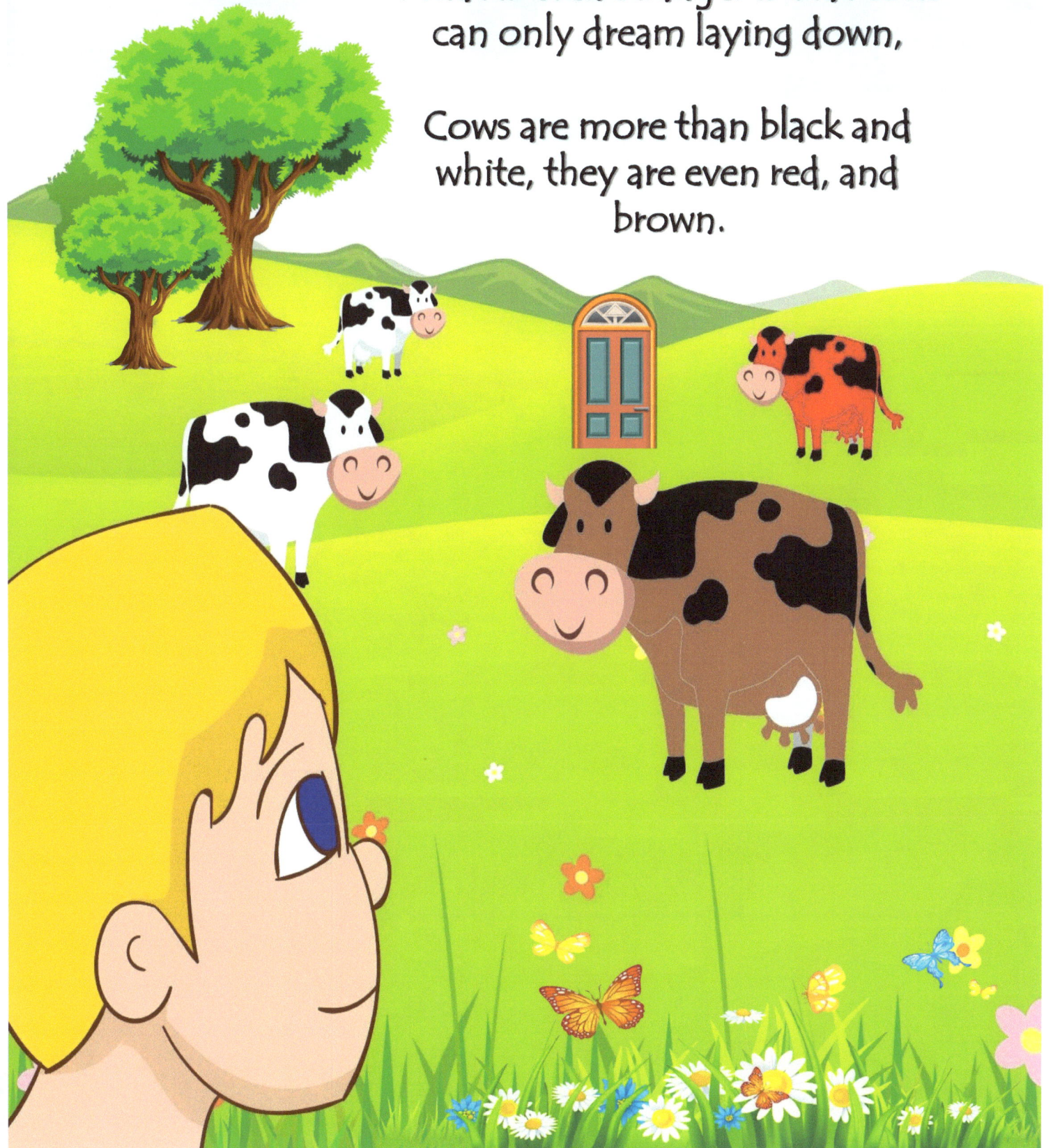

Ezra saw many doors,
but they all needed a key,
except for one,
which could that be?

Not many options to choose from unless he was
smart,
One door is fine for now, it is a start.

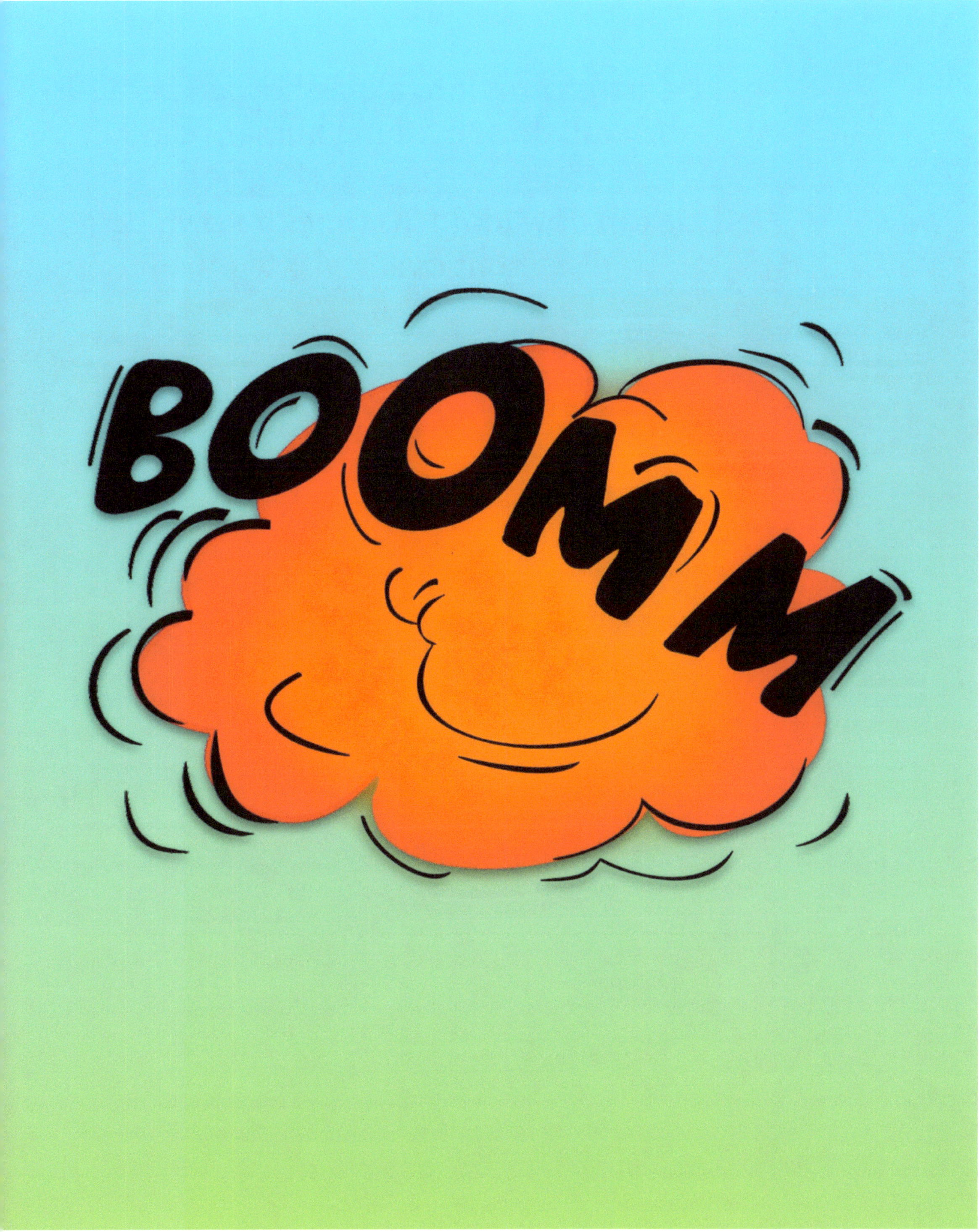
BOOMM

Ezra transforms into a grasshopper, because
they can do something humans can't...

Ezra can now jump 20 times his own body,
right over a plant.

Compared to a kid
at a height of 5 feet,

It's like a human
jumping 100 feet,

Over a building,
and landing back on
the concrete.

Ezra saw many doors,
but they all needed a key,
except for one,
which could that be?

Not many options to choose
from unless he was smart,
One door is fine for now,
it is a start.

Ezra is now a Hippo,
so much bigger than his mom,

She asked to race,
with confidence Ezra was calm!

Ezra said,
"I know as a Hippo I could win the race,"
So Ezra ran at a very fast pace.

Ezra saw many doors,
but they all needed a key,
except for one,
which could that be?

Not many options to choose
from unless he was smart,
One door is fine for now,
it is a start.

THIS WAY
THAT WAY

Hello Ezra! My name is Timmy The Toucan.

I have been watching you as you became so many things,

I can see a lot from up here, with these big beautiful wings.

What have you learned so far? Any news?

Now that you tried on their shoes!

Yes of course!

A cow sleeps standing, but only dreams laying down,

Cows are more than black and white, they are even brown,

Grasshoppers can jump 20 times the length of their own size...

Hippos can outrun humans, so it's important not to judge and to be wise.

Ezra stops his daydream, and looks at the door,

He use to think that school was such a bore,

But now he's changed,
and he wants to learn more.

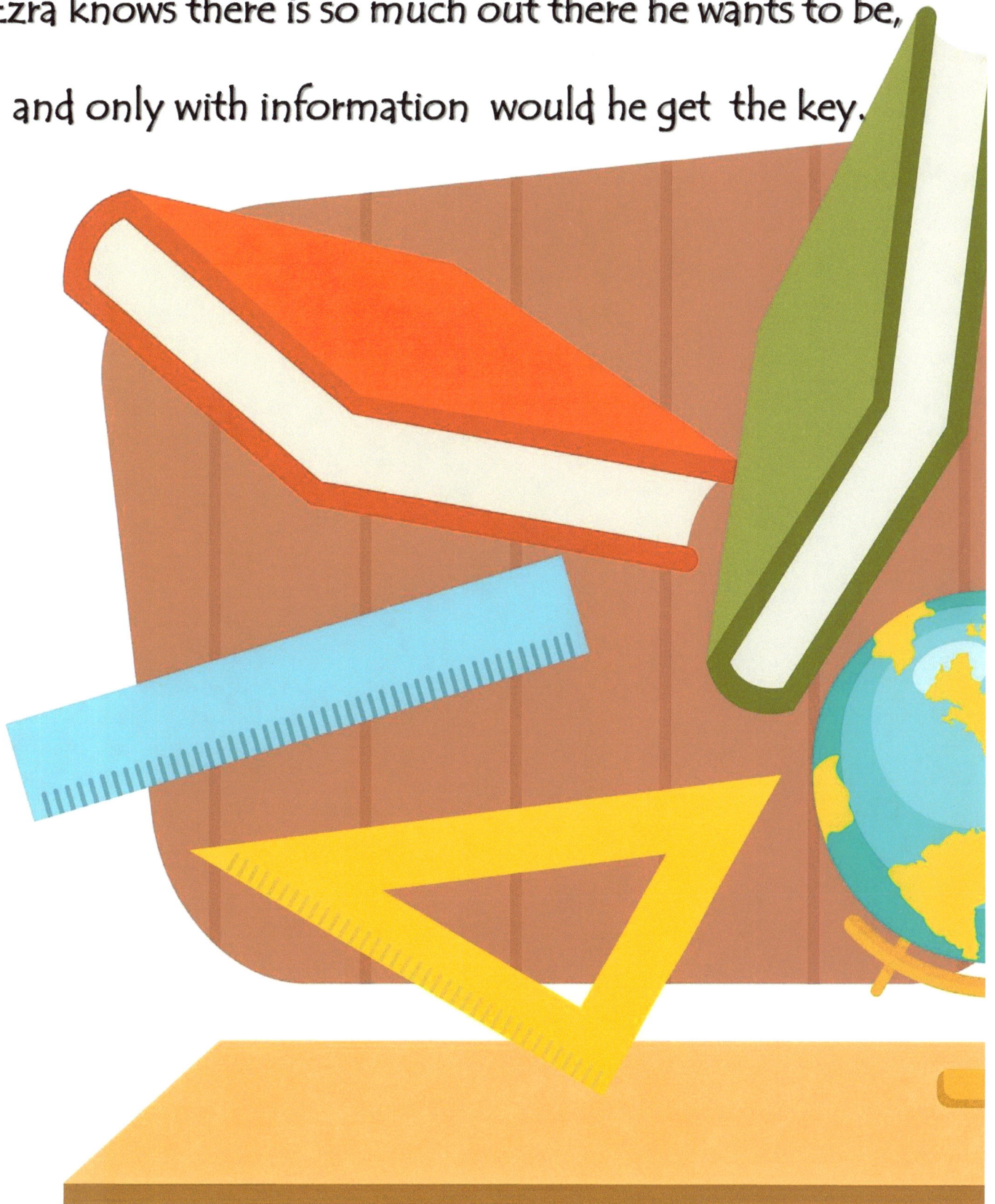

Ezra knows there is so much out there he wants to be,

and only with information would he get the key.

Ezra learned so much, while having fun,

Ezra always stayed humble, and respected everyone.

THE END

Questions You May Ask!

What are some morals you have learned?

In what ways do you think you are like Ezra?

If you where an animal, which would you be? And why?

www.ingramcontent.com/pod-product-compliance
Lightning Source LLC
Chambersburg PA
CBHW041556040426
42447CB00002B/196